Compiled by Helen H. Moore

Illustrated by Jacqueline B. Levin

To my mother-in-law,
Rose Castellano Sorvillo
who was wise enough, long ago,
to know how much a young
daughter-in-law needed her love

Book design by Arlene Greco

202 Mamaroneck Avenue
White Plains, NY 10601

ISBN 0-88088-089-9
Printed in China
7 6 5 4 3 2 1

Wise Women
Said
These Things

– *Introduction* –

It is known that girls, in general, begin to speak at an earlier age than boys. And it seems we maintain this verbal advantage over the opposite sex as we grow up, and for the rest of our lives, as well. Which is wonderful, because, for one thing, it means that there is so much "woman's wisdom" in the culture, passed down from mother to daughter, written from friend to friend, spoken or dramatized by actresses and politicians, and published by scholars, journalists, and authors!

Maybe it's because of the nature of the lives we lead—endlessly intersected by the joys and sorrows of the cycles of love and loss—

women have always felt the need to express ourselves in words . . . and to listen to each other, too.

In fact, throughout history, wise women have had so much to say that, in collecting the quotations for this book, the only difficulty has been in deciding what to leave *out.*

The women represented on the pages of this book don't always agree, in substance or in style, except in one way: each one is, was, or has been, in her own fashion, a Wise Woman.

- H. H. M. -

omen Said These Things Wise Wo

ise Women Said se Th

Things

Said These

Women Said These

Women Said

gs Wise Women Said These Things Wise Wo

ings Wise Women Said

gs Wise Women Said These Th

To Begin With

We are all born charming, fresh and spontaneous and must be civilized before we are fit to participate in society.

Judith Martin (Miss Manners)

There is a wonderful word—*Why?* that children, all children, use. When they stop using it, the reason too often is that no one bothered to answer them. No one fostered and cultivated the child's innate sense of the adventure of life.

Eleanor Roosevelt

If I'm too strong for some people, that's their problem.

Glenda Jackson

People often claim that a particular behavior is "natural" and "biological" when they don't want to change it.

Harriet Lerner

Even my different drummer heard a different drummer.

Florence King

A Simple Request:

Don't interrupt me when I'm eaves-dropping.

Jacqueline Susann

Ain't I a Woman?

If the first woman God ever made was strong enough to turn the world upside down all alone, these women together ought to be able to turn it back, and get it right side up again!

Sojourner Truth

A woman can withstand everything.

Coco Chanel

Modern invention has banished the spinning wheel, and the same law of progress makes the woman of today a different woman from her grandmother.

Susan B. Anthony

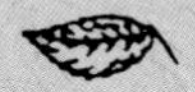

How simple a thing it seems to me that to know ourselves as we are, we must know our mothers' names.

Alice Walker

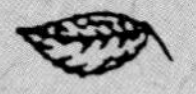

A woman's best protection is a little money of her own.

Clare Boothe Luce

Women are not little children.
Women are not weak, not victims.
Pleasure and danger go together,
of course they do. We want the
pleasure, and we can cope with
danger.

Nadine Strossen

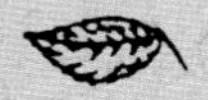

One is not born, but rather becomes,
a woman.

Simone de Beauvoir

omen Said These Things Wise Wo

ise Women Said These Th

These Things Wise Women

Things Said These

Things Wise Wom

Wise aid These

Women Said

gs Wise Women Said These Things Wise W

ings Wise Women Sai

gs Wise Women Said These Th

Men and Women: The Great Divide

When a woman behaves like a man why doesn't she behave like a *nice* man?

Edith Evans

Why should we assume that if men talk too much and try to dominate the agenda, we can't tell them to pipe down? How is it that men can be environmentalists, and men can be antiracists, but somehow, magically, men cannot, equally legitimately, be feminists?

Naomi Wolf

Lipstick is power.

attributed to *Barbara Follett*

It's so much easier for men. They don't have to paint their nails for a meeting.

Eve Pollard

In politics, if you want anything said, ask a man. If you want anything done, ask a woman.

Margaret Thatcher

Women are accused of being catty, but really, think about it: when two women meet, they will usually say something to each other like, "I love your hair that way," or "That color looks great on you;" something nice. When two men friends meet, on the other hand, they say things to each other like, "Nice suit . . . does it come in your size?"

Liza Charlesworth

Stereotypes defend the borders of gender, but they can't effect separation between the sexes. Masculinity and femininity may stand on either side of a mile-high wall, yet women and men share beds and homes, histories and children.

Judith Levine

Growing up, I was a daddy's girl. I can still recall the way he called me to come into the house from play some evenings, extending the final syllable of my middle name in his deep Tennessee drawl. . . . Only in recent years have I begun to understand fully how powerful that relationship was in shaping every area of my life.

Dorothy Gilliam

Boyfriends are right at your side at the snap of your fingers. They hover over you trying to anticipate your every desire. My husband used to be like that. Nothing I wanted inconvenienced him. When we were dating, I asked him to drive to Cincinnati to get me a doughnut. He did it. When, during a blizzard, I asked him to get me an ice cream cone, he said, "What flavor?" He doesn't do that anymore.

Merlene Davis

Both men and women are fallible. The difference is, women know it.

Eleanor Bron

The research on hormones and aggression suggests we would do well to shift our primary attention from progesterone to testosterone. High testosterone in men has been linked to antisocial behavior such as delinquency and substance abuse, but that hasn't made headlines . . . why [do] we have a syndrome called PMS but not one called HTS—Hypertestosterone syndrome?

Harriet Lerner

On the Other Hand . . .

It is hard to resist a man who sings to you, or sends you violets, or braids your hair, and even an invitation to a pool game and a bowl of soup afterward can be magic when it comes from a man you can enchant.

Merle Shain

Wise Women Said These Things

Wise Women Said These Things

Wise Women Said These Things

Wise Women Said These Things

JOURNAL

On Love

Do you want me to tell you something really subversive? Love *is* everything it's cracked up to be.

Erica Jong,
How To Save Your Own Life

LOVE has nothing to do with what you are expecting to get—only with what you are expecting to give—which is everything.

Katharine Hepburn,
Me

It's afterwards you realize that the feeling of happiness you had with a man didn't necessarily prove that you loved him.

Marguerite Duras

What is Love? Love is . . .

A warm and tender smile
A sudden rush of feeling
Walking the extra mile
What sets your heart a-reeling
Holding hands in moonlight
A sudden burst of sun
High emotion and pure delight
Two hearts entwined as one.

Nicole Beale

Only love can be divided endlessly and still not diminish.

Anne Morrow Lindbergh

If all of us just loved and cared for one person each. That is all it takes. Love breeds love. Maybe then we will be able to prevent each other from going insane. Maybe then we will be able to prevent each other from becoming violent, as violence is in our hearts and not in our weapons. Guilt is not in the one who pulls the trigger, but in each of us who allows it.

Yoko Ono
letter to the press, after the murder of John Lennon in 1980

No love is entirely without worth, even when the frivolous calls to the frivolous and the base to the base.

Iris Murdoch

omen Said These Things Wise WomenS

ise Women Said These Thing

These Things Wis en

e Things

men Said These omen S

W Said These T

gs Wise Women Said These Things Wise Wome

hings Wise Women Said

gs Wise Women Said These Thin

Said These Things Wise W

The Mating Game

One of the oldest human needs is having someone to wonder where you are when you don't come home at night.

Margaret Mead

There you are you see, quite simply, if you cannot have your dear husband for a comfort and a delight, for a breadwinner and a crosspatch, for a sofa, a chair or a hotwater bottle, one can use him as a Cross to be borne.

Stevie Smith

A husband is what's left of the lover once the nerve has been extracted.

Helen Rowland

The perfect mate, despite what "Cosmopolitan" says, does not exist, no matter how many of those tests you take.

Suzanne Britt Jordan

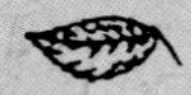

There is a rule in sailing where the more maneuverable ship should give way to the less maneuverable craft. I think this is sometimes a good rule to follow in human relationships as well.

Dr. Joyce Brothers

Marriage resembles a pair of shears, so joined that they can not be separated; often moving in opposite directions, yet always punishing anyone who comes between them.

Sydney Smith

Even a long and happy marriage has some years, even some decades, that are happier or more fulfilling than others.

Nicole Beale

"M" IS FOR . . .

Motherhood is the strangest thing, it can be like being one's own Trojan horse.

Rebecca West

If you bungle raising your children, I don't think whatever else you do matters very much.

Jacqueline Kennedy Onassis

I was also very affected by the first time I felt the baby kick. And yet it wasn't a kick at all, which is what I had been led to expect, but a flickering, like a little butterfly alive in my belly.

Sophia Loren

To me, life is tough enough without having someone kick you from the inside.

Rita Rudner

Take motherhood: nobody ever thought of putting it on a moral pedestal until some brash feminists pointed out, about a century ago, that the pay is lousy and the career ladder nonexistent.

Barbara Ehrenreich

It goes without saying that you should never have more children than you have car windows.

Erma Bombeck

Kids don't stay with you if you do it right. It's one job where, the better you are, the more surely you won't be needed in the long run.

Barbara Kingsolver

Do not, on a rainy day, ask your child what he feels like doing, because I assure you that what he feels like doing, you won't feel like watching.

Fran Lebowitz

The word *no* carries a lot more meaning when spoken by a parent who also knows how to say *yes*.

Joyce Maynard

I love children. Especially when they cry—for then someone takes them away.

Nancy Mitford

I long to put the experience of fifty years at once into your young lives, to give you at once the key of that treasure chamber every gem of which has cost me tears and struggles and prayers, but you must work for these inward treasures yourselves.

Harriet Beecher Stowe

omen Said These Things Wise Won

ise Women Said These Th

These Things Wise Women

Things Women Said These T

nen Said These Things Wise Wome

Wise Women Said These

Women Said

gs Wise Women Said These Things Wise Wo

ings Wise Women Said

The "D" Word . . .

Moving from marriage to divorce is like traveling to a foreign country. Few of us are eager for the journey; few can afford the fare; and few know how to cope en route or what to expect when we arrive.

Eleanor Dienstag

I envy people who have the capacity to sit with another human being and find them endlessly interesting. I would rather watch TV. Of course, this eventually becomes known to the other person.

Carrie Fisher,
Postcards from the Edge

If the second marriage is a success the first one really isn't a failure.

Mignon McLaughlin

When Life Hands You Lemons . . .

When sorrow and loss and conflict are overwhelming, bake a pie.

Sister Helen Prejean,
Dead Man Walking

The harder they hit, the more encouraged I get.

Hillary Rodham Clinton

Conscience and Character

Characters live to be noticed. People with character notice how they live.

Nancy Moser

The path upon which we have set our course is not an easy one. The trail is often difficult to find. We must make our maps as we go along, but we travel in good company with men and women of good will in the free countries of the world.

Eleanor Roosevelt

I cannot and will not cut my conscience to fit this year's fashions.

Lillian Hellman

Vomen Said These Things Wise Wo

Vise Women Said These Th

d These Things Wise Wome

se Things Said These

omen Said These Things

Wise Women Thes

se Women Said

ngs Wise Women Said These Things Wise

Things Wise Women Sa

ings Wise Women Said These

THE UNHOLY TRINITY: DIETING, FASHION, AND BEAUTY

Buying something on sale is a very special feeling. In fact, the less I pay for something, the more it is worth to me. I have a dress that I paid so little for that I am afraid to wear it. I could spill something on it and then how would I replace it for that amount of money? Tell me that.

Rita Rudner

Any girl can be glamorous: all you have to do is stand still and look stupid.

Hedy Lamarr

The prospect of being feminine always makes me think of James M. Cain's reply when asked to write for *The New Yorker*: "On the whole, I'd rather be dead."

Florence King

Elegance is not a matter of slipping into a new dress. You're elegant because you're elegant, a new dress has nothing to do with it. You can be elegant in a skirt and jersey.

Coco Chanel

I'm tired of all this nonsense about beauty being only skin-deep. That's deep enough. What do you want, an adorable pancreas?

Jean Kerr

I told myself, "Oprah, be a good sport. This man must know what he's doing." What he did was burn my hair right off. I felt the lotion burning my skull, and I kept saying, "Excuse me, this is beginning to burn a little." They kept saying, "Oh, just a few more minutes." Within a week all [my] hair fell out: You learn a lot about yourself when you're bald.

Oprah Winfrey

On Modern Life

Television is actually closer to reality than anything in books. The madness of TV is the madness of human life.

Camille Paglia

I think television has been rough on even the hardiest of us. It shows us beautiful people that we'll never look like, riches that we'll never attain, and excitement that we'll never experience. And no wonder, because so little of it is reality.

Marilyn vos Savant

"You cannot become a better person through massage!"

Jennifer Saunders,
from *Absolutely Fabulous* television series

The telephone is a good way to talk to people without having to offer them a drink.

Fran Lebowitz

There is no need to go to war. Not now we've got fax machines.

Sue Townsend

Did You Ever Notice . . .

Humor is a spontaneous, wonderful bit of an outburst that just comes. It's unbridled, it's unplanned, it's full of surprises.

Erma Bombeck

There are three ways to get something done: do it yourself, employ someone or forbid your children to do it.

Monta Crane

What I don't get is: why is there war, why is there pollution, why is there starvation and why do guys quit liking you when you start liking them?

Lynda Barry

If one is lucky, a solitary fantasy can totally transform one million realities.

Maya Angelou

There are no shortcuts to any place worth going.

Beverly Sills

The Spirit of Things . . .

The very core of what I believe is this concept of individual worth, which I think flows from all of us being creatures of God and being imbued with a spirit.

Hillary Rodham Clinton

Every wish is like a prayer with God.

Elizabeth Barrett Browning

If man is only a little lower than the angels, the angels should reform.

Mary Wilson Little

Throughout our lives, we are brought in contact with spiritual advisors; the trick is not in meeting them, but in recognizing them when we do.

Erica Jong

I read the book of Job last night—I don't think God comes well out of it.

Virginia Woolf

There is nothing in this world quite so wonderful as the faith a child has in one they love.

"Calamity Jane"
(Martha Jane Burk)

GIRLFRIENDS

The connections between and among women are the most feared, the most problematic, and the most potentially transforming force on the planet.

Adrienne Rich

Even friends I haven't seen in years are still with me, though we no longer sit on one another's kitchen counters on Saturday mornings. The letters and phone calls over the years aren't just biding time till the next visit; sometimes they are the friendship.

Kathryn Stechert Black

For fifty years there has been an unbroken friendship between us. . . . We did not agree on every point, but on the central point of woman suffrage we always agreed. . . . I cannot express myself at all as I feel, I am too crushed to speak. If I had died first, she would have found beautiful phrases to describe our friendship, but I cannot put it into words. She always said she wanted to outlive me so that she could give her tribute to the world.

Susan B. Anthony,
on the death of Elizabeth Cady Stanton

omen Said These Things Wise Women

ise Women Said These Thin

Wise Women Said These Things Wise Won

hings Wise Women Said

gs Wise Women Said These Thi

Sisters, Sisters . . .

We have gathered as we often did in those pink rooms to tell our stories—to share our surprise at the women we have become—to talk about the way we were as girls and the way we are now.

bell hooks

For when three sisters love each other with such sincere affection, the one does not experience sorrow, pain, or affliction of any kind, but the others' heart wishes to relieve, and vibrates in tenderness. Like a well-organized musical instrument.

Elizabeth Shaw,
sister of Abigail Adams
and Mary Cranch

It is true that I was born in Iowa, but I can't speak for my twin sister.

Abigail Van Buren,
Dear Abby

We often call each other to bare our souls. Sometimes I call her to vent about issues she knows absolutely nothing about, but it's a safe environment to do that. And she does it as well.

Barbara Ross-Lee,
sister of Diana Ross

The Big Three: Work, Money, Success

The two most beautiful words in the English language are "Check Enclosed."

Dorothy Parker

If you ask me to name the proudest distinction of Americans, I would choose the fact that they were the people who created the phrase "to *make* money." No other language or nation had ever used these words before; men had thought of wealth as a static quantity—to be seized, begged, inherited, shared, looted or obtained as a favor. Americans were the first to understand that wealth has to be created.

Ayn Rand,
Atlas Shrugged

To fulfill a dream, to be allowed to sweat over lonely labor, to be given a chance to create, is the meat and potatoes, of life. The money is the gravy.

Bette Davis

I always go where the dough is.

Gypsy Rose Lee

Nobody gets to live life backward. Look ahead—that's where your future lies.

Ann Landers

Keep a diary and one day it'll keep you.

Mae West

Women are too much inclined to follow in the footsteps of men, to try to think as men think, to try to solve the general problems of life as men solve them. The woman is not needed to do man's work. She is not needed to think man's thoughts. Her mission is not to enhance the masculine spirit, but to express the feminine. Hers is not to preserve the man-made world, but to create a human world by the infusion of the feminine element into all of its activities.

Margaret Sanger

There is a time for work, and a time for love. That leaves no other time.

Coco Chanel

The trouble with being in the rat race is that even if you win, you're still a rat.

Lily Tomlin

All good fortune is the gift of the gods, and . . . you don't win the favour of the ancient gods by being good, but by being *bold*.

Anita Brookner

The only way we can totally protect ourselves from humiliation is by not trying to do anything challenging. But if we want to try to succeed on a grand scale, we take the risk of criticism on a grand scale.

Harriet Lerner

Lots of people want to ride with you in the limo, but what you want is someone who will take the bus with you when the limo breaks down.

Oprah Winfrey

s Wise Women Said

men Said These Things Wise Wom

se Women Said These Thi

These Things Women

Thi men Said These T

en Said These ngs men

Wis Wo en Sai These

Women Said

s Wise Women Said These Things Wise Wo

ngs Wise Women Said

CALL *THAT* PROGRESS?

If they could put one man on the moon, why can't they put them all?

Unknown

GROWING UP IS HARD TO DO

A child who is protected from all controversial ideas is as vulnerable as a child who is protected from every germ. The infection, when it comes—and it will come—may overwhelm the system, be it the immune system or the belief system.

Jane Smiley

Life is a Mystery . . .

You never know why you're chosen to be an instrument.

Rosalind Russell

There are two ways of spreading light: to be the candle or the mirror that reflects it.

Edith Wharton

If the world were a logical place, men would ride side-saddle.

Rita Mae Brown

The heart is the toughest part of the body. Tenderness is in the hands.

Carolyn Forché

People from a planet without flowers would think we must be mad with joy the whole time to have such things about us.

Iris Murdoch

The great secret: *To hold on, let go. Nothing is solid. Everything moves. Except love—hold on to love. Do what love requires.*

Sister Helen Prejean,
Dead Man Walking

Because you suddenly realize what a tremendous opportunity it is just to be alive. The potential. If you can keep a-goin'—you actually can do it. So just keep a-goin'—you can win. It's when you stop that you're done.

Katharine Hepburn

MOTHERHOOD, *REDUX*

Becoming a grandparent is a second chance. For you have a chance to put to use all the things you learned the first time around and may have made a mistake on. It's all love and no discipline. There's no thorn in this rose.

Dr. Joyce Brothers

A nice thing about grandchildren is you can tell them stories about "olden times" and they'll never question the details.

Margery Eliscu

e Women Said These Thi

hese Things Wise Women

Things Wise Women Said These Th

n Said These Women

hese

Women Said

s Wise Women Said ngs Wise Wom

ngs Wise aid

Wise Women Said These Thi

AGING

I hate faces that have no questioning in them, no quest for wanting to learn more, see more, *be* more!

Maria Tallchief

One of the many things nobody ever tells you about middle age is that it's such a nice change from being young.

Dorothy Canfield Fisher

We grow neither better nor worse as we get old, but more like ourselves.

May Lamberton Becker

The "I should" of the twenties, which gives way to the "I want" of the thirties, becomes the "I must" of the forties.

Gail Sheehy,
Passages

Old age is like a plane flying through a storm. Once you are aboard there is nothing you can do.

Golda Meir

You don't get to choose how you're going to die. Or when. You can only decide how you're going to live. Now.

Joan Baez

I remembered how carefree I used to be with my body. It never occurred to me that I might break something or that anything could go wrong at all. Now I had to think ahead even when I got out of a taxicab.

Shirley MacLaine,
Out on a Limb

Women Said These Things Wise Women

Wise Women Said These Thin

These Things Wise Women

e Things

se Thi

Th

The

nen

se

e Said

ngs Wise Women Said These Things Wise Wom

Things Wise Women Said

ngs Wise Women Said These Thin

Said These Things Wise W

The best remedy for those who are afraid, lonely or unhappy is to go outside, somewhere where they can be quite alone with the heavens, nature and God. Because only then does one feel that all is as it should be and that God wishes to see people happy, amidst the simple beauty of nature. As long as this exists, and it certainly always will, I know that then there will always be comfort for every sorrow, whatever the circumstances may be. And I firmly believe that nature brings solace in all troubles.

Anne Frank,
The Diary of a Young Girl

Looking Back

Education matters. Kindness matters. Truth matters. Patience, hard work, tolerance, discipline—all of these matter. Forgiveness matters and gratitude matters . . .

Hillary Rodham Clinton

And, in the End . . .

Even if you're wracked by troubles, and sick and poor and ugly, you've got your soul to carry through life like a treasure on a platter.

Alice Munro